To:

_____
_____
_____
_____

From:

_____
_____
_____
_____

Date:

_____

COPYRIGHTS AND ACKNOWLEDGMENTS:

Copyright © 2015 by Q. M. Herrera / Blessed Inspirations 33, LLC

Blessed Inspirations - The Greatest is Love/Q.M. Herrera. -- 1st ed.
ISBN 978-0-9970359-3-3

All rights reserved. No part of this publication may be reproduced, distributed or transmitted in any form or by any means, without prior written permission.

Blessed Inspirations 33, LLC
Post Office Box 471236
Kissimmee, FL 34747-9992
www.blessedinspirations33.org

Royalty-free images retrieved with permission through the following resources:

Fotolia (2015) https://us.fotolia.com
Pixabay (2015) https://pixabay.com

Bible Scriptures referenced herein were retrieved from Bible Gateway at www.biblegateway.com, from the following versions:

The Holy Bible, New International Version (NIV) Holy Bible, New International Version®, NIV® Copyright ©1973, 1978, 1984, 2011 by Biblica, Inc.® Used by permission. All rights reserved worldwide.

World English Bible (WEB)
by Public Domain. The name "World English Bible" is trademarked.

Blessed Inspirations

THE GREATEST IS LOVE

by Q. M. Herrera

BLESSED INSPIRATIONS 33, LLC

"This book is a clean fountain of inspiration that brings us to the knowledge of the Divine Love. Each message is a song of gratitude and praise that invites the soul to enter into communion with God. It is certainly an extraordinary work of deep spirituality and a celebration of life."

-Ruben Dario Hoyos Alegria
Best-Selling Author of *The Power of Faith*
International Motivational Speaker

"This is a powerful, moving and beautiful book that will bring inspiration to many."

-Jessica Walters
Prayers and Apples

PREFACE

    This is a personal collection of poems, lyrics, prayers and meditations, which were divinely inspired to bring peace, light, love and inspiration to all, regardless of religious denomination, age, race or gender. During this special spiritual journey, I drew upon my life experiences in order to relay my innermost feelings and reflections on faith, hope, love and life. I also express my deepest gratitude and appreciation, through joyful praises to our God, the Creator of Heaven and earth, for His presence and all the wonderful blessings He has bestowed upon me.

    I pray that the blessings and meditations contained herein will uplift your heart and be useful in your spiritual journey. May this book also serve as a great gift of love, joy and peace for your friends and loved ones.

Q. M. Herrera

TO MY BELOVED ANGELS AND SAINTS
IN HEAVEN AND ON EARTH

AND

TO GOD, MY CREATOR,
THE SOURCE OF LOVE, LIFE AND
ALL MY INSPIRATION

"*But now faith, hope, and love remain—these three. The greatest of these is love.*"

—1 Corinthians 13

Contents

INTRODUCTION: LIFE IS A JOURNEY 1
PART 1: THE GIFTS OF LIFE AND LOVE 9
    Love Is All Around 19
    My Favorite Things 25
    The Greatest Is Love—Part 1 33
    The Greatest Is Love—Part 2 39
SPECIAL DEDICATION 43
PART 2: FATHER AND SHEPHERD 45
    To My Angels, With Love..53
    Until We Meet Again 59
    The Lord Is My Shepherd 65
    God of Comfort 69
    Your Presence 73
PART 3: MEDITATIONS OF THANKS AND PRAISE 79
    Come Holy Spirit 81
    Give Thanks To The Lord 87
    Rejoice and Be Glad 91
    Come To The Table 95
    Because of You 101
    Amazing God 105
    My Dear Jesus 109
    Prayer of Thanksgiving 111
PART 4: FAITH AND SWEET SURRENDER 115
    In God's Time..123
    The Lord Is My Light 129
    I Believe..133
    My Beloved...137
    Let Your Light Shine 141

INTRODUCTION: LIFE IS A JOURNEY

Life is a journey…

To find love,
To find peace,
To find happiness;

Life is a journey…
To find our destiny,
To find our life's purpose,
To find God and
To become One with our Creator.

Life truly is a journey. We find ourselves constantly searching for knowledge and hungry for information that will help us become wise, but wisdom is not acquired automatically. In this lifetime, we will meet people and encounter many experiences that will serve as great inspiration and building blocks in our growth as individuals. I have learned that we must live our lives, make mistakes, and even suffer losses and heartaches, in order to grow and learn from those experiences. Those experiences, not only help us become wiser over time, but they reveal hidden qualities, gifts or talents about ourselves that we perhaps overlooked or did not realize that we possessed all along.

Our lives continue to evolve each day and we never stop learning. Although the truth may hurt at times, we must go through certain experiences, which allow us to face the truth about ourselves, including truths about the people, relationships and circumstances in our lives. By facing these truths and seeing things more clearly, we are then able to execute change for our better good, resulting in the achievement of peace and true happiness.

*"Be still, and know that I am God.
I will be exalted among the nations.
I will be exalted in the earth."*
　　　　　　　　　　—Psalm 46:10

Our experiences, whether good or bad, help mold us into the people that we are today. There are times that God allows us to go through certain experiences in order to be redirected onto the right path or help us change our expectations and perspectives. As a result, we are able to focus on the things that are truly important and help us fulfill our life's purpose.

It is important to remember, however, that one should never give up hope. We must remain faithful and keep our hearts and minds open in order to receive the wonderful blessings that God has in store for each one of us. *God communicates with us in many different ways, but we must slow down and be still long enough to hear His messages.*

If we remain open-minded, faithful and surrender ourselves to God, we will find that the answers have been placed deep within our hearts all along. Moreover, it is in those times of sweet surrender that God does His greatest work and performs miracles in our lives.

I have found that it is not always easy to maintain a positive perspective when there are countless examples in the media about the cruelty that exists in this world. On the other hand, *we are surrounded by many things that remind us of all that is <u>good</u> and the many blessings God has bestowed upon us.*

If we take a moment to look around us, we will see evidence of God's love and presence — in all of God's creations, life, love, kindness, compassion, laughter, special moments spent with family and friends, and much more.

> *"We are surrounded by many things that remind us of all that is <u>good</u> and the many blessings God has bestowed upon us."*

This certainly coincides with the notion that pertains to the existence of God and the devil, and the difference between good and evil. I prefer to err on the side of all that is good, peaceful and kind, and strive to be the best possible version of the person God created me to be in order to fulfill His purpose for me.

For these reasons, I have decided to share the wonderful inspirations that God has placed in my heart. I truly believe that with God there are no coincidences. If you are reading this book, it is because there is a special blessing for <u>*you*</u>.

THANK YOU for your support and for joining me on this special journey.

*I pray that the writings contained
herein will uplift your heart and
serve as inspiration for you;
May your heart be filled with God's
Grace, Love and Joy; and
May God, our Father and Creator,
Bless you forevermore!
In the name of God the Father,
the Son and the Holy Spirit,
Amen!*

PART 1: THE GIFTS OF LIFE AND LOVE

"What no eye has seen, what no ear has heard, and what no human mind has conceived—the things God has prepared for those who love him."

—*1 Corinthians 2:9*

W e live in an imperfect world. A world filled with sorrow, poverty, sickness, war and discord. A world filled with evil and sin. The thing is... God loves us so much that He created us in His image. Yet, we are all unique individuals with our own imperfections. It is our individuality, however, that makes us beautiful. Even with these imperfections, each person is special and loved by God.

Every individual possesses a certain level of beauty, both seen and unseen. Each person has been blessed with the gift of life and other gifts or talents, of which the person may or may not be aware. Additionally, these gifts come in many different forms.

For example, some people may be born with the creative gifts of singing, dancing, writing or speaking. Some people are born to become athletes, serve in the armed forces, become firefighters or policemen; some are meant to be great leaders, parents or caregivers; some may have the gift of being good listeners or counselors; and some people are born with the ability of bringing joy and laughter to others. The list can go on and on.

"God is love and the source of all life. Love is of God and every living creature on this earth, including you and I, represent the great care and love that God put forth in all of His creation."

If we take a moment to take a look at ourselves and the world around us, we will begin to see that beyond all the pain, misery, sorrow and sickness, *there is much beauty and we have been blessed with so much more — life and love.*

Let's take a moment to think about the air we breathe each day. We can't see it, but without it, we would cease to exist. What about all the beautiful things in nature — trees, plants, flowers and animals — as well as the sun, moon, stars, ocean and mountains? As you can see, it only takes a moment or two to realize that we are surrounded by so much life, love and beauty, and we are truly blessed.

If you have never read *The Story of Creation* (Genesis 1), I highly recommend that you do so. It is so inspirational and depicts how much love and care God put forth in creating the heavens and the earth, including all that surrounds us in the earth and humankind.

God is love and the source of all life. Love is of God and every living creature on this earth, including you and I, represent the great care and love that God put forth in all of His creation. As God completed each phase in the process, He paused, reviewed His work and saw that it was <u>good</u>. How wonderful it must have felt to have that sense of accomplishment and being truly happy with one's creation and work!

Every living creature on this earth was created to serve a specific purpose and maintain balance in accordance with God's plan. Thus, we are loved beyond measure and there is so much more God has in store for those who love Him (1 Corinthians 2:9).

> *"I know the plans I have for you," declares the LORD, "plans to prosper you and not to harm you, plans to give you hope and a future."*
>
> *—Jeremiah 29:11*

In fact, from the beginning of time and on many occasions throughout history, God has proven His never-ending love and mercy. God has also demonstrated that He created humankind with the intention that we live a life filled with love, peace, harmony, prosperity and righteousness. Such examples are depicted in the biblical stories of *The Story of Creation* (Genesis 1), and *Noah's Ark and The Flood* (Genesis 5).

However, the greatest example of love occurred when God sacrificed His only Son, Jesus Christ, so that we may be forgiven and have everlasting life (i.e., saved from eternal damnation).

> *"For God so loved the world, that he gave his one and only Son, that whoever believes in Him should not perish, but have eternal life."*
>
> —John 3:16

As such, I cannot think of a greater, more unconditional love than this. Can you?

When we experience difficult times, it is not easy to maintain a positive perspective on things, especially when we feel alone, sad, discouraged, abandoned, betrayed or distressed. However, I have learned that even in the midst of tragedy, there is always a blessing awaiting in disguise. These blessings are God's way of reminding us of His love and presence. These blessings are also reminders of the importance of maintaining a connection/personal relationship with God.

There are times that we may not be able to see the blessing immediately or understand why certain things are happening in our lives. Nonetheless, I found that it is important to keep an open mind in order to receive the blessings that God has for us. One should also remember that God manifests His love in different ways.

"For He will put His angels in charge of you, to guard you in all your ways."

—Psalm 91:11

> *"No matter what happens in this lifetime, we are never alone."*

I found that God sends wonderful surprises when least expected and needed the most. During our life's journey, there are times we may feel alone and discouraged, but when least expected, we are showered with the gifts of love, compassion, comfort and peace through friends, loved ones and even complete strangers. I believe that these strangers are Angels in disguise!

As you may see, God loves us so much that He assigned Heavenly Angels to watch and guide each one of us. Now, that is a lot of Angels! Whether we listen or take heed to the messages, that is another story.

With that being said, remember that no matter what happens in this lifetime, *we are never alone.* We are valued and loved beyond measure by our God and Master of all creation! I truly believe in God's never-ending and unconditional love. Just like the air that I breathe each day, I would not be able to live without God's love, mercy and guidance. Time and time again, God makes His presence known and never ceases to amaze me.

I am so thankful for God's love and all the blessings that He continues to bestow upon me each day. I am also very thankful for the Heavenly Angels that God has charged to watch over every living creature on this earth, including you and I.

TO GOD BE THE GLORY!

LOVE IS ALL AROUND

"Love brings peace to the weary, and light in the darkness."

Love is all I have ever wanted,
Love is all I have ever needed;
I believe in love, and
I believe in you.

Love is all around us,
It heals the wounded and
warms the coldhearted;
Love brings peace to the weary,
and light in the darkness.

Love is the air that we breathe,
and the essence that gives us life;
For without it, we can't survive.
Love is having faith and giving your heart;
Love doesn't give up, but gives us hope.

Love is the sun, the moon and the stars;

Love conquers all,

No matter how great or small.

Love is the Breath of Life,

Coming down from Heaven;

Love is God and all of His creation.

Love is the smile that we give to one another;
    Love is when we give a helping hand to a stranger;
        God is Love, and
            we are loved by our Creator.

God makes His presence known every day;
    He took His time and created us in His image;
Just open your eyes and open your heart,
    And you will see that God is Love, and
        Love is of God.
            We are loved and
                LOVE IS EVERYTHING!

MY FAVORITE THINGS

Flowers blooming on the first of May,
A cool breeze on a hot summer day;
Sharing and fellowship amongst family and friends,
A friend who listens and truly understands.

Waking up to sounds of birds singing in the morning,

    Light after darkness and a new day that is dawning;

Catching a beautiful sunset at the beach in the evening,

    Exchanging gifts "just because" and for no special reason.

Spring, Summer, Winter and Fall,

    Leaves falling and turning colors in the Fall;

Families and friends sharing moments together,

    Creating special memories that will be treasured forever.

Couples holding hands and walking in the park,

    Looking at the moon and stars after dark;

A couple falling in love as they look into each other's eyes,

    Having great conversation over a glass of wine.

People smiling, laughing, spending time together,

    Friends gathering, no matter the time or weather;

The sharing of ideas, feelings and views,

    Listening to music and dancing to the groove.

Laughing out loud and enjoying the simple things,

Thanking God for each day and all His blessings!

THE GREATEST IS LOVE—PART 1
(Inspired by 1 Corinthians 13)

"But now faith, hope, and love remain —these three. The greatest of these is love."

—1 Corinthians 13

Love is beautiful and love is forever. For as long as I am able to remember, 1 Corinthians 13 has been my favorite scripture because it describes the characteristics of true love: *patience, kindness, trust, faithfulness, humility, honesty, forgiveness, faith, hope and perseverance.* Although this scripture is often recited at weddings, the words contained therein remind us of the manner in which we should treat one another, regardless of relationship. Love applies to everyone and all types of relationships, whether those relationships are amongst friends, families, co-workers, courtships, marriages, etc.

God created us and understands that no one is perfect. As such, we should not expect perfection from anyone because it is not humanly possible. However, we can strive to become the best versions of ourselves and do right by others. There are many other biblical scriptures that refer to love, but this one in particular has always stood out to me and reminds me of how beautiful love truly is!

"Beloved, let us love one another, for love is of God; and everyone who loves has been born of God, and knows God."

—1 John 4:7

I truly believe in love and will never give up on love. Love is a precious gift that comes from heaven and should be treasured. We may attain all the desired worldly possessions, riches and successes in this lifetime, *but without love, we are nothing.*

It is important to remember that you and I were created in the image of our Creator. As such, you and I are part of God and we also represent the essence of His love. Love comes from God and love is the essence of God. Therefore, love is forever and certainly is the greatest gift of all!

THE GREATEST IS LOVE—PART 2
(Inspired by 1 Corinthians 13)

Love is patient, Love is kind,

    Love is a flame that turns darkness into light;

    Love is beautiful, Love is grand,

Love is a miracle that no one understands.

Love is not jealous, boastful or rude,

    Love is humble and rejoices in the truth;

Love is faithful, Love is pure,

    Love always trusts, hopes and endures.

    Love, Love, Love…

        God is Love and Love is of God;

        Now these three remain:

            Faith, Hope and Love;

THE GREATEST IS LOVE.

Love is an Angel that makes us feel secure,

    Love is the Spirit of God and this I know for sure;

God is Love and it's what we've been yearning,

    God's Love is faithful and never-ending.

Love is like the ocean, too deep to comprehend,

    Love is a friend who listens and is with you till the end;

Love is God's Spirit that lingers long,

    It is the song you want to sing so loud and strong.

    Love, Love, Love…

        God is Love and Love is of God;

            Now these three remain:

                Faith, Hope and Love;

                THE GREATEST IS LOVE.

Love is a gift that comes from Heaven,

    Love is more valuable than any possession;

Love is our destiny and God's promise forever,

    LOVE NEVER FAILS.

    Love, Love, Love…

        God is Love and Love is of God;

            Now these three remain:

                Faith, Hope and Love;

THE GREATEST IS LOVE.

SPECIAL DEDICATION

The following poems and meditations are

dedicated to my beloved family,

especially my beautiful sons,

Kevin and Anthony,

and

our precious loved ones who are no

longer with us and whose memories will

be held in our hearts forever.

PART 2: FATHER AND SHEPHERD

"Like a shepherd guarding his sheep, God protects and keeps watch over us. Whenever we are lost or have gone astray, God awaits with open arms for His children to come home to Him."

When one becomes a parent, we want the best for our children. During pregnancy, the expectant mother is careful about what she eats and eats nutritious meals so that the unborn child receives the best nutrients while he or she is developing in the mother's womb. After the baby is born, the parents continue to take good care of the child and do all that is within their means to educate and protect the child from harm.

This level of care continues throughout the life of the child. Even when the child becomes an adult, the parents never stop caring, worrying and desiring the best for their sons and daughters. *In the same token, God loves all His children, big and small, from the youngest to the eldest, regardless of age, color or gender.*

God wants the very best for all His children and created this world with the intention that we live in peace and harmony with one another, and that we live a life of plenty--a life filled with love, happiness, prosperity and freedom from oppression.

"God loves all His children, big and small, from the youngest to the eldest, regardless of age, color or gender."

Unfortunately, the corruption of sin has tainted this world and it is filled with much sadness, distress, oppression, war, poverty and hunger. People often want to question or blame God for their troubles, but God did not impose or cause these things to occur in this world. Man did this, not God.

In *The Story of Creation* (Genesis 1), it is evident that God created a paradise that included everything that we needed to live healthy, plentiful, peaceful and happy lives. The entire universe and every living creature, including you and I, was created beautifully and with much care to ensure that everything was balanced.

> *"For you formed my inmost being. You knit me together in my mother's womb. I will give thanks to you, for I am fearfully and wonderfully made."*
>
> —*Psalm 139:13-14*

It is not God's fault that man has disobeyed God, time and time again. However, every individual has free will and has the option to do the right things and live in accordance with God's commandments. God understands that we are human and have our limitations. We will make mistakes along the way, but God is a loving, forgiving and merciful father. He knows what we hold in our hearts and knows us better than anyone.

> *"Life is truly a miracle and must be protected, safeguarded and treasured."*

Like a shepherd guarding his sheep, God protects and keeps watch over us. Whenever we are lost or have gone astray, God awaits with open arms for His children to come home to Him.

I have loved my sons since before they were born. I will never forget the times they were born and the first time I held them in my arms. Each time I looked into their eyes and held them, I fell in love with them over and over again. *Life is truly a miracle and must be protected, safeguarded and treasured. We must do everything within our means to protect the lives of the innocent and the environment in which we live.*

The love of a parent is unique and very special, and is usually not understood until one becomes a parent. Although I knew that my sons would grow up one day, I was certainly not prepared to let them go. However, I have embraced this new chapter in our lives and look forward to the wonderful blessings that God has in store for us.

With that being said, I am very thankful to God for blessing me with the gift of motherhood. No matter where life leads us and no matter what happens in this lifetime, I will love and cherish my sons forever.

Thank you, God, for blessing me

with the wonderful gifts of

Life and Love.

Thank you for my family and

for the gift of motherhood.

Thank you for always taking care of me

and for never leaving my side.

I love you, my Lord and God, and

Bless Your Holy Name!

TO MY ANGELS, WITH LOVE

"Behold, children are a heritage of Yahweh. The fruit of the womb is His reward."

—Psalm 127:3

As I look up at the sky, the moon and many stars,
I think of my loved ones and wonder how they are;
God knows my daily struggles and what is in my heart,
I love my friends and family, although we are apart.

I look back and have thoughts of my childhood,
When I dreamt of the future — marriage and motherhood;
God has blessed me, indeed, with two little Angels,
And for that I am truly and forever grateful.

My two little Angels are all grown up,
I am so proud of the men they have become;
One is a U.S. Marine defending our country,
The other an actor, singer and martial artist.

As you live your life each day, I hope you will remember,

    Enjoy every moment, for life is short and must be treasured;

Remember to love and honor God above all things,

    And no matter what happens in life,

Be thankful for all your blessings!

Life is filled with many choices and it won't always be easy,

    Trust God and what's in your heart, choose your path wisely;

Love and respect yourself as well as those around you,

    The Holy Spirit that lives within you will always guide you.

I pray that you live your life to its fullest potential,

    God has a plan and we all have a purpose to fulfill;

Live, love, laugh out loud and enjoy the simple things,

    Life is what we make it, and

        It is filled with endless possibilities.

You are always in my thoughts, and

    I thank God for you each day;

    I pray that God blesses and keeps you out of harm's way.

So, as you embark on your life's journey,

    I hope you will remember;

        That I hold you close to my heart, and

            Will love and cherish you forever!

UNTIL WE MEET AGAIN
(Inspired by Luke 23:43)

"Today you will be with Me in Paradise."

—Luke 23:43

In this lifetime, we will suffer losses. It is very painful to lose the people that we love and we will hold the memories of our loved ones forever in our hearts. When we suffer these types of losses, they tend to create a void in our hearts and no matter how much time lapses, there is a longing in our hearts--to see them, hold them, hug them once more. There is also a longing to hear the person's voice once again.

I know these feelings very well because I, along with my family members and many people in this world, have suffered losses that occurred suddenly and during a short period of time. I long to see my loved ones and there are times I just want to be able to say hello and have a conversation with them, but I realize that the longing I feel in my heart can never be filled by anyone or any worldly possession. Only God is able to fill the void and provide the peace that we have been longing for in our hearts.

It has been ten years since my mother passed away, and over time, I have begun to gain a better understanding of my mother's desire to be with the Lord. My mother suffered with cancer for many years and longed to be with the Lord because she believed in His promise that one day, we will be with Him in paradise — a place where there is no suffering, a place filled with pure love, beauty and peace.

> *"God created me and my entire being belongs to the Lord, my Creator. Without God, I am nothing."*

Although we are made of flesh and bones, we must remember that we are spiritual beings. There are times I have felt displaced, as though I don't quite fit in, and realize that it is because my spirit is not of this world. *God created me and my entire being belongs to the Lord, my Creator. Without God, I am nothing.*

We are all born with the inherent need to be loved and feel a sense of belonging. As such, we were created to live in communion (to be one) with God. I have found that it is important to maintain a special connection with God because it is through that connection that I am able to feel God's love and presence in my life. It is also through my personal relationship with God that I am able to gain peace, understanding and wisdom.

It is extremely difficult to let go of our loved ones, but our time on this earth is limited and all life is in God's hands. I would prefer to have my loved ones near me at all times, but also realize that God is a merciful God. I am able to attain a sense of peace knowing that they are no longer suffering and in a place of rest.

The longing to see my loved ones once again will never cease, but I truly believe in God's promises that one day we will be reunited in paradise.

Farewell, My Darlings...
The time has come to say farewell
and I hate to let you go;
I hold you close to my heart,
I miss you and love you so.
Thank you for the love and beautiful
memories we shared;
Life has not been the same without you.
I only say farewell, My Darlings...
for one day we will be reunited in Heaven;
Farewell, My Darlings...
Until we meet again.

THE LORD IS MY SHEPHERD
(Inspired by Psalm 23)

"The Lord is my shepherd, I shall not want."

—*Psalm 23*

The Lord is My Shepherd, I shall not want,
    He leads me to quiet waters;
        He quenches my soul and is always by my side,
    The Lord is my Shepherd and there is nothing I shall want.

You lead me through green pastures and are always by my side;
    You keep me safe and guide me to the path of righteousness.
In moments of distress, you comfort and give me peace;
    You hold me in the palm of Your hands.

The Lord is My Shepherd, I shall not want,
    He leads me to quiet waters;
He quenches my soul and is always by my side,
    The Lord is my Shepherd and there is nothing I shall want.

The Lord is my Shepherd, there is nothing I shall not want,
    In the still of the night, He watches over me;
In the valley of the darkness, I shall have no fear,
    The Lord is my Shepherd and watches over me.

The Lord is My Shepherd, I shall not want,
     He leads me to quiet waters;
He quenches my soul and is always by my side;
     The Lord is my Shepherd and there is nothing I shall want.

You prepare a table for me before my enemies,
     You anoint my head with oil and my cup overflows;
Your love is always with me all the days of my life,
     I will dwell in the house of the Lord forever!

GOD OF COMFORT
(Inspired by 2 Corinthians 1:3-4)

God of Comfort, Spirit of Light,
    Be with me always, this day and night;
    I raise Your Name in praise,
Alleluia to the Name of All Names.
    I bless Your Holy Name, Alleluia.

God of Power, God of Might,
    I am yours and You are mine;
You are my comfort and joy,
    Alleluia to The Song of All Songs.
I bless Your Holy Name, Alleluia.

You are Holy, Holy, Alleluia,
    You are worthy of all praise;
For You came into this world,
    To wash away all sin,
And bring us to eternal life;
    I bless Your Holy Name,
        Alleluia, Alleluia.

God of Mercy, My Lord and God,
    Heavenly Father, God of All Creation;
You alone are The Holy One,
    Alleluia to The King of All Kings;
I bless Your Holy Name, Alleluia.

You are Holy, Holy, Alleluia,
    You are worthy of all praise;
For You came into this world,
    To wash away all sin,
And bring us to eternal life;
    I bless Your Holy Name,
        Alleluia, Alleluia.

For unto us a child is born, unto us a Son is given,
    All darkness and sin has been forgiven;
Wonderful Counselor, Almighty God,
    Everlasting Father, Prince of Peace.

My Sweet God of Glory,
    You're The Name of All Names;
        Blessed Savior, Sweet Lamb of God,
            Blessed Redeemer, Emmanuel.

    I BLESS YOUR HOLY NAME,
        ALLELUIA.

YOUR PRESENCE

"You will show me the path of life. In Your presence is fullness of joy. In Your right hand there are pleasures forevermore."

—Psalm 16:11

When I feel alone and can't stop the tears from falling,

You send me words of wisdom to see that a new day is dawning;

When things seem too hard to bear and no one is around who cares,

You hold me in Your arms and let me know You care;

    You let me know that You are always there.

No matter what happens in life,

You are here in good times and bad;

    "There's no need to worry," You say,

    "There's need to feel sad."

You send me a gentle breeze to let me know that You are near;

    "Like a warm embrace, I am with you;

    Always, my Dear!"

My God, You let me know that You are always near;

You let me know that You are always here.

Your presence is like the sun, shielding us from the darkness,
    Your presence is like the moon and stars at night;
Your presence is like a gentle breeze flowing through the air,
    Giving us peace and comfort, like a friend who really cares.

Your presence is like the sun, giving light to see,
    That through Your Son, Jesus, we have the victory!
I thank you, Lord, 'cause you are always there.

    Thank you, Lord, for Your presence.
        Thank you, Lord, in the daytime.
            Thank you, Lord, in the nighttime.
            Thank you, Lord.

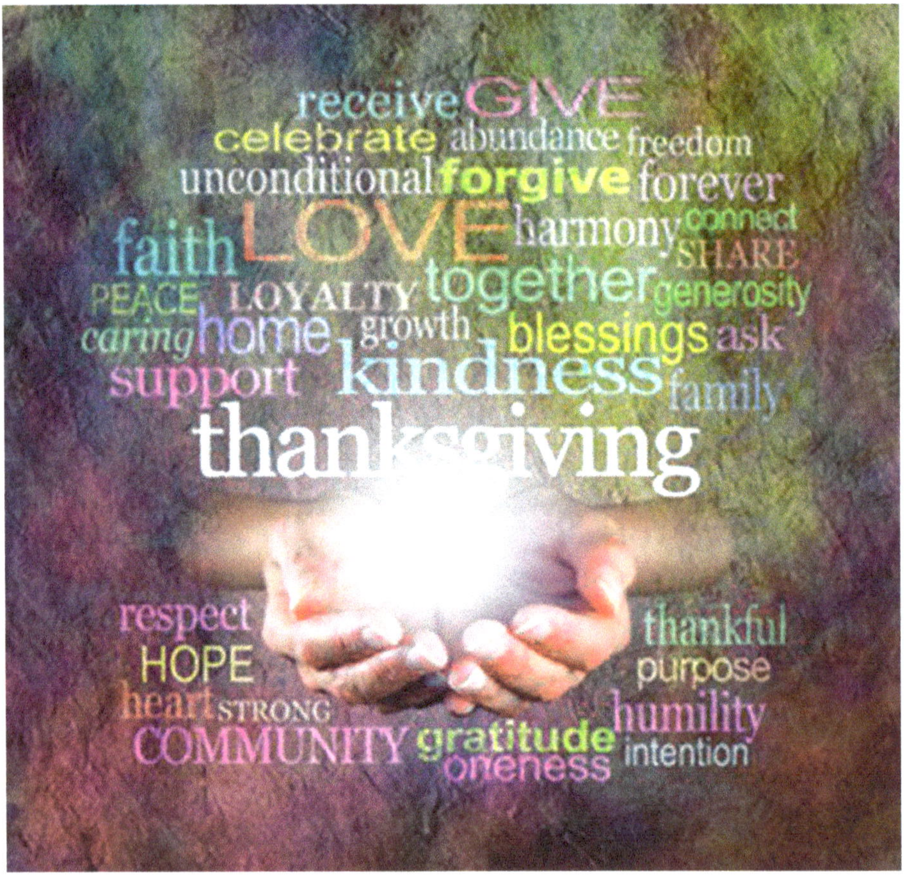
receive GIVE
celebrate abundance freedom
unconditional forgive forever
faith LOVE harmony connect
SHARE
PEACE LOYALTY together generosity
caring home growth blessings ask
support kindness family
thanksgiving
respect
HOPE
heart STRONG
COMMUNITY gratitude
oneness
thankful
purpose
humility
intention

PART 3: MEDITATIONS OF THANKS AND PRAISE

"You send out Your Spirit and they are created. You renew the face of the earth."

—Psalm 104:30

COME HOLY SPIRIT
(Inspired by Psalm 104:30)

Come Holy Spirit, Come!
Fill us with Your grace and power,
Fill us with Your peace and light, Holy Spirit;
Come Holy Spirit, Come!

Come Holy Spirit, Come!
    Come and fill the hearts of Your faithful;
Fill us with the fire of Your love, Holy Spirit,
    and renew the face of the earth.

Send forth Your Spirit, make me new,
    Fill me with the fire of Your love;
Come Holy Spirit,
    Fill me with Your light,
and create in me a clean heart, oh God.

Come Holy Spirit, Come!
    Fill us with your grace and power,
Fill us with Your peace and light, Holy Spirit;
    Come Holy Spirit, Come!

Come Holy Spirit, Come!
    Come and fill the hearts of Your faithful;
Fill us with the fire of Your love, Holy Spirit,
    and renew the face of the earth.

Come Holy Spirit,
    Fill me with Your power,
Give me courage and
    peace in my darkest hour;
Holy Spirit, fill me with Your knowledge,
    Help me to be faithful and truly wise.

Come Holy Spirit, Come!
    Fill us with your grace and power,
Fill us with Your peace and light, Holy Spirit;
    Come Holy Spirit, Come!

Come Holy Spirit, Come!
    Come and fill the hearts of Your faithful;
Fill us with the fire of Your love, Holy Spirit,
    and renew the face of the earth.

May your light shine upon me
    for the whole world to see
        that Jesus, Your Son, has removed all
    darkness and fear; Alleluia!

Come Holy Spirit, Come!

    Fill us with your grace and power,

Fill us with Your peace and light, Holy Spirit;

    Come Holy Spirit, Come!

Come Holy Spirit, Come!

    Come and fill the hearts of Your faithful;

Fill us with the fire of Your love, Holy Spirit,

    and renew the face of the earth.

"Give thanks to the Lord, for He is good; His love endures forever."

—Psalm 118:1

GIVE THANKS TO THE LORD
(Inspired by Psalm 118:1)

Give thanks to the Lord for He is good;
His mercy and love endures forever.

Thank You, my Lord, for Your presence,
In moments of despair, You give me refuge;
I proclaim to all the nations,
The wonders of the Lord;
God's love and mercy is everlasting!

Give thanks to the Lord for He is good;
His mercy and love endures forever.

Thank You, my Lord, for Your presence,
You heard my cry and You answered me;
The Lord is my Shepherd, God and Redeemer,
The Lord is my strength and song;
He is my salvation!

Give thanks to the Lord for He is good;
    His mercy and love endures forever.

I will shout for joy and proclaim,
    What the Lord has done for me;
The stone the builders rejected,
    Has become the cornerstone;
This is the day the Lord has made,
    Let us rejoice and be glad!

Give thanks to the Lord for He is good;
    His mercy and love endures forever!

"This is the day that the Lord has made. We will rejoice and be glad in it!"

—Psalm 118:24

REJOICE AND BE GLAD
(Inspired by Psalm 118:24)

Rejoice and be glad for a new day has come,
　　Rejoice and be glad, we have a chance to start anew;
A day of laughter, peace and joy,
A day of new life, faith and hope;
Let us rejoice, be glad and give thanks,
　　Alleluia! We have the victory!

Rejoice and be glad, sing glory and praise,
　　To our Redeemer and Name of all Names;
New life, new hope to all He brings,
　　Glory and praise to our Risen King!

Sing to the Lord and shout for joy,
　　Raise your voices in praise and thanksgiving;
This is the day the Lord has made,
　　Let us rejoice and be glad!

Rejoice and be glad for a new day has come,
Rejoice and be glad, we have a chance to start anew;
    A day of laughter, peace and joy,
    A day of new life, faith and hope;
Let us rejoice, be glad and give thanks,
    Alleluia! We have the victory!

Rejoice, be glad and give thanks to the Lord,
    Praise Him with tambourines and dancing;
Make a joyful noise to the Lord, all the earth,
    For He is good and His love endures forever!

Rejoice and be glad, our Savior has come,
    All darkness and sin has been forgiven;
He has turned our mourning into dancing,
    I praise and bless Your Holy Name,
Alleluia!
    Holy, Holy, Holy is His Name!

Rejoice and be glad to our merciful God,
    For the wonderful gift of salvation;
He is worthy of all glory and praise,
    Jesus Christ has risen today;
Alleluia! We have victory!
    Alleluia, Alleluia, Alleluia, Amen.

Rejoice and be glad, our Savior has come,
    Holy, Holy, Holy is God's name;
Heaven and earth are full of His glory,
    Hosanna in the Highest!

Rejoice and be glad for a new day has come,
Rejoice and be glad, we have a chance to start anew;
    A day of laughter, peace and joy,
    A day of new life, faith and hope;
Let us rejoice, be glad and give thanks,
Alleluia! We have the victory!

COME TO THE TABLE

He took bread, gave thanks and broke it, and gave it to them, saying, "This is My body given for you; do this in remembrance of Me."

—Luke 22:19

Come to the table of our Lord,
    All are welcome, come as you are;
    United in prayer and united we sing,
To praise our Savior and Risen King;
Rejoice, be glad and give thanks!
    We have the victory!

Gather at the feast that our Lord has made,
    Eat of the bread and drink of the wine;
"Do not be afraid and do not be ashamed,
    For I love you and you are mine."

"Eat of this bread for this is My Body,
    All who are hungry shall hunger no more;
All who are tired, weak and distressed,
    Lay down your burdens and come find your rest."

"Drink of this cup for this is My Blood,

    All who are thirsty shall thirst no more;

Trust in Me for I have paid the price,

    So that you will not perish, but have Eternal Life!"

Come to the table of our Lord,

    All are welcome, come as you are;

United in prayer and united we sing,

    To praise our Savior and Risen King;

Rejoice, be glad and give thanks!

    We have the victory!

"Eat this bread and drink of this cup,

    This is My Body, this is My Blood;

The Blood of the Covenant that I shed for many,"

    So rejoice, be glad and give thanks,

For we have the victory!

"Come to Me, all you who labor and are heavily burdened, and I will give you rest."

—Matthew 11:28

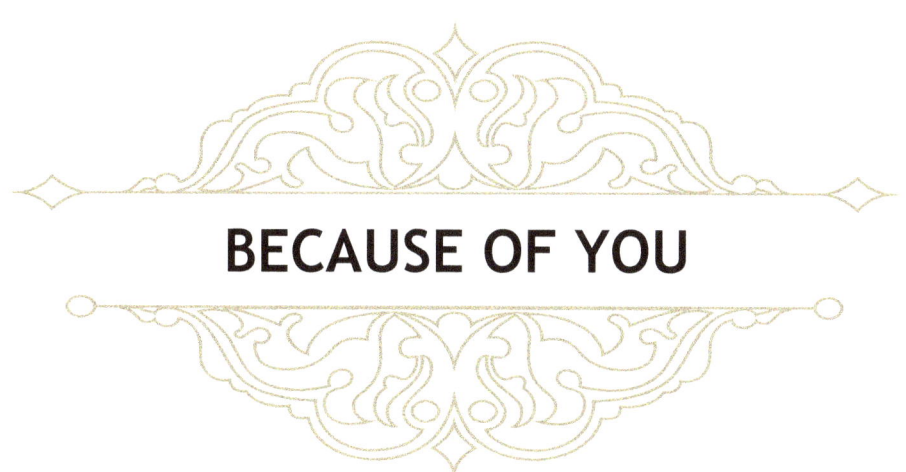

BECAUSE OF YOU

Looking at my life and all the years gone by,
Thinking about yesterday and tomorrow;
There's been good times, pain and sorrow,
but through it all, I have been Blessed.

Because of You, I am free,
    Because of You, I am alive;
Because of You, I have been redeemed,
    and because of You, I am free to be ME.

Life can change unexpectedly,
    and it can feel like a broken Halleluiah;
but even in those times, there are lessons to learn,
    and there are blessings in disguise.

Because of You, I am free,
    Because of You, I am alive;
Because of You, I have been redeemed,
    and because of You, I am free to be ME.

For these reasons I sing glory and praise,
      to the Almighty King;
For these reasons I bless His Holy Name,
      for He is alive and has conquered death;
and I sing Halleluiah.

Because of You, I am free,
      Because of You, I am alive;
Because of You, I have been redeemed,
      and because of You, I am free to be ME.

AMAZING GOD

"You have searched me, Lord, and You know me. You know when I sit and when I rise; You perceive my thoughts from afar."

—Psalm 139:1-2

You are my amazing God,
    And all that I aspire to be;
    How precious are Your works, Oh God,
    I praise You for Your blessings and;
All that You have done for me!

You search me, Lord, and You know me,
    You know when I sit and when I rise;
You know my heart and thoughts from afar,
    Nothing can escape from You.

You are my amazing God,
    And all that I aspire to be;
How precious are Your works, Oh God,
    I praise You for Your blessings and;
All that You have done for me!

Where shall I go from Your Spirit?
    Your presence is always with me —
You are the air that I breathe,
    And the light in the darkness.

You are my amazing God,
    And all that I aspire to be;
How precious are Your works, Oh God,
    I praise You for Your blessings and;
All that You have done for me!

You are my Lord, God and Savior
    The Father, the Son and Holy One,
        You are the Lamb; and
            You are The One and only,
                Great, I AM.

MY DEAR JESUS

My Dear Jesus:

My thoughts and prayers are with You today and every day. You came into this world in loving sacrifice in order to fulfill the command of our Father, God and Creator.

You, who were born without sin and God's only son, performed many miracles while You were on this earth. You healed the sick and brokenhearted, gave sight to the blind, fed multitudes of people that were hungry, converted souls and much more.

Yet, You were judged, betrayed, ridiculed, abused, rejected, denied, abandoned, treated like a criminal and condemned to death. You wore a crown of thorns and carried the cross up to Calvary. You suffered and bore all our burdens in silence and never complained. While being nailed to the cross, You did not think about yourself and Your only concern was our salvation.

You suffered all these things and died for me so that I may be free and have everlasting life. I love You, Lord, and thank You for all You have done and all You continue to do each day for me.

Your loving servant,

Q. M. Herrera

PRAYER OF THANKSGIVING

Thank You, God of all creation,
    You are the source of life and all inspiration;
    Thank You, Lord, for this brand new day,
You are worthy of all glory and praise.

Thank You, Lord, for all Your blessings,
    and for all that You do;
Thank You for Your presence,
    and for never leaving my side.

Thank You for Your guidance every day of my life;
    Whenever I feel lost or dismayed,
You always hold my hand and help me find my way.

Thank You, God, for all that You do,
 And thank You for all that You are;
You created the heavens and the earth,
 And saw that it was good;
You created us in Your image and saw the good in us;
 Even when we fail, You continue to have hope and faith in us.

Thank You for Your forgiveness and mercy;
 Thank You for Your unconditional love.
You are my rock and salvation,
 You are the stronghold of my life.
My life is in Your hands,
 I put my trust and faith in You;
For You are love, life and all that is good.
 You are beautiful and all that I aspire to be;
 You are my light and I praise Your Holy Name.

  Alleluia!

I praise you in the morning;
    I praise You in the night, and
I praise You at all times;
    You are worthy of all glory and praise; and
I bless Your Holy Name.

Thank you for saving me and for believing in me.
    Most of all, thank You for Your Love and Grace.
Without You, I am nothing but a clashing cymbal.
    You are always at my side and never forsake me.

You are my amazing God;
    You are my partner, most loyal friend and confidant.
You are my all and all.
    Thank you, my Lord and my God!

        Amen!

PART 4: FAITH AND SWEET SURRENDER

"*For we live by faith, not by sight.*"

—*2 Corinthians 5:7*

I grew up in a very religious home and am very thankful that I had the opportunity to learn about God during my childhood. I have wonderful memories of attending parochial school, singing in the school and church choirs, and being involved in the youth group.

As the years have passed, I have realized that the seeds of faith that were planted during my youth, have remained with me and my faith has been an essential part of my life. Although I have always had faith in God, I am human and there are times that my faith has been tested. I have spent most of my life taking care of others and always tried to be strong for others' sake.

During difficult times, I never allowed my children or most people to see my cry. I would smile and tell everyone that all is okay, but I realized that I was trying to bear much more than I was able handle by myself. There were times that I felt heavily burdened and overwhelmed.

One day, I realized that I did not have to be strong all the time. God knows my limitations and it is okay to be human. Everyone has the right to grieve and feel emotions, such as fear, anger, sadness and joy. We do not have to carry our burdens alone and it is okay to admit when we need help.

When Jesus died on the cross in Calvary, He carried our burdens in order for our sins to be forgiven and so that we may have eternal life. As such, God wants us to live a life of peace. There is no need to spend our energies worrying about things or trying to carry our burdens alone because Jesus has triumphed over death and has paid the price for us.

Moreover, Jesus reminds us that He wants us to come to Him and cast our burdens so that He will give us rest.

> *"Come to Me, all you who labor and are heavily burdened, and I will give you rest."*
>
> —*Matthew 11:28*

As I was waking up one Saturday morning, I remembered hearing the words, *"consider the lilies of the field and how they grow."* The words sounded familiar and I wondered what God was trying to tell me. I remembered singing a song that contained that phrase when I was in the high school choir. I tried searching for the song, but could not find it.

I ended up getting busy with my day. Several hours later (when I got settled in for the night), I remembered those words again. After conducting some research on the Internet, I was ecstatic to figure out what God was trying to tell me by reading Matthew 6:25-34, titled *"Do Not Worry"*.

> *"Why do you worry...? Consider the lilies of the field, how they grow; they neither toil nor spin."*
> —Matthew 6:28

In Matthew 6:25-34, God reaffirms that He does not want us to worry about anything (food, drink, clothing, etc.). God knows exactly what we need and knows our thoughts and deepest desires. Just as God has taken care of the lilies and grass in the field, God will always take care of those who seek His kingdom and righteousness (Matthew 6:33).

Furthermore, God does not want us to spend our energies worrying about tomorrow because tomorrow will bring its own level of worries, burdens and anxieties (Matthew 6:34). If we remain faithful and put our focus on God, all will be given to us.

"Delight yourself in the Lord and He will give you the desires of your heart."

—Psalm 37:4

Faith can move mountains. I truly believe that, with faith, we are able to achieve more than we can ever imagine. It takes great courage to overcome one's fears and take that leap of faith. It may be difficult to let go of control, but time and time again, I am reminded that God is in control of everything. It is also not easy to step out of one's comfort zone and let God take the wheel, sort to speak, but I must say that from my own personal experiences, it is in those moments of surrender that God truly makes His presence known. It is in those moments of sweet surrender that God does His greatest work and performs miracles in our lives.

As a dear friend once told me, *"God's timing is a strange thing, but when you let go of the wheel and allow Him to drive, you can sit back and enjoy the ride."* She is absolutely right! When we surrender all our fears and worries to God, we allow the real healing and transformation to take place within ourselves — spiritually, mentally and physically — and God is able to transform our lives in ways that we are not able to imagine.

Remember, however, that when we decide to let go, this does not mean that our faith will not be tested and things will be easy. There are times things in our lives must be broken apart for God to do His work and put the pieces back together where they belong. There are times situations will arise that become opportunities for us to change our focus, put us back on track or simply steer us in the right direction. We must also remember to trust in God's intervention and that everything happens in accordance with God's plan and, therefore, everything has a time and purpose.

"For everything there is a season, and a time for every purpose under heaven."

—*Ecclesiastes 3:1*

IN GOD'S TIME

There are various points in my life where I had my share of concerns and experienced moments of loneliness, despair and losses. One evening, I heard the words, *"Don't Worry"* and in that moment I realized that God does not want me to worry about anything. I remembered that God has always taken care of me and has never let me down. God reminded me that, *"For everything there is a season, and a time for every purpose under heaven"* (Ecclesiastes 3:1).

Suddenly, my worries turned into laughter. I started chuckling because I heard the Beatles' song in my head, *"...for everything... turn, turn, turn... there is a season... turn, turn, turn."* In that moment, I realized that even being single during this time of my life has a purpose and is part of God's divine plan for me.

God has allowed me this time to work on realizing my dreams and goals. It is a time to focus on God and allow Him to guide me in the direction He wants me to follow. It is about taking that blind leap of faith and knowing that, no matter what, God always has my back and will always take care of me. So, what do I have to worry about? Nothing! Nothing at all.

With that being said, we should keep in mind that we belong to God and everything we receive is a gift from God. We must continue to be thankful each and every day for all of God's blessings, even during the difficult times. We must also continue to work on improving ourselves and making whatever changes are necessary to do God's will and fulfill our life's purpose.

I realize that God is empowering me with the courage, wisdom and understanding that is needed to make a difference in other people's lives. My life experiences will not only serve as learning tools for myself, but are testaments of the manner in which God has performed miracles and intervened in my life. So, I end this chapter by reciting the following words that God has placed in my heart:

> *"Do not be discouraged when things do not go your way. I AM HERE and will never forsake you. All will transpire at the time and place that has been predestined for you. I know what is in your heart. I know what you desire and what you need. I hold you in the palm of My hands."*

*Thank You, Lord,
for all Your blessings.
Thanks to all
the Heavenly Angels and Saints
for keeping me company
and helping me with God's plan.
May it all be for
God's glory and praise,
Amen!*

"The Lord is my light and my salvation - whom shall I fear?
The Lord is the stronghold of my life - of whom shall I be afraid?"

—Psalm 27:1

THE LORD IS MY LIGHT
(Inspired by Psalm 27)

The Lord is my light and salvation, my deliverer,
　　Whom shall I fear? Whom shall I fear?
　　The Lord is the stronghold of my life;
　Of whom shall I be afraid?

I love You, Lord; You are my strength,
　　You are my light and refuge;
You saved me from my enemies and set me free,
　　You are righteous and faithful.

The Lord is my light and salvation, my deliverer;
　　Whom shall I fear? Whom shall I fear?
The Lord is the stronghold of my life;
　　Of whom shall I be afraid?

I will praise You, LORD, among the nations,
    I'll sing praises to Your name;
You rescued me because You love me,
    I praise Your Holy Name. Alleluia!

The Lord is my light and salvation, my deliverer;
    Whom shall I fear? Whom shall I fear?
The Lord is the stronghold of my life;
    Of whom shall I be afraid?

Thank You, God of all creation,
    You are my life and all inspiration;
I put my trust and faith in you,
    My life is in Your hands.

The Lord is my light and salvation, my deliverer;
    Whom shall I fear? Whom shall I fear?
The Lord is the stronghold of my life;
    Of whom shall I be afraid?

I BELIEVE

I believe in a God that is alive,
    whose Holy Spirit lives within us;
    I believe in God the Father,
Creator of Heaven and earth;
    I believe in the seen and unseen.

I believe in Jesus Christ,
    the only Son of the Father,
who walked this earth
    and performed many miracles.

He fed the hungry, and
    turned water into wine;
He healed the sick,
and gave sight to the blind;
    He converted many souls,
and showed us how to pray:

Our Father who art in heaven,
Hallowed be Your Name;
Thy Kingdom come, Thy will be done,
on earth as it is in heaven.
Give us this day our daily bread,
Forgive us our trespasses;
as we forgive those who trespass against us.
Lead us not into temptation, but
deliver us from the evil;
For thine is the Kingdom, the power, and
the Glory are Yours forever.
Amen!

-Matthew 6:9-13

MY BELOVED

My Beloved, my Sweet God of Glory;

Thank You for the courage to share my story.

Heavenly Father, Prince of Peace,

You fill my soul with sweet melodies;

For when I am lost or feel dismayed,

You hold my hand and help me find my way.

Whenever I feel lonely and in times of despair,

My Heavenly Father is always there;

God has a plan and a purpose for my life,

He will not leave or forsake me,

But lead me on the right path.

Heavenly Father, Prince of Peace,

    You fill my soul with sweet melodies;

I thank You for Your blessings, each day and night,

    For I am yours and You are mine.

God of comfort, my Lord and my God,

    Name of All Names and Song of All Songs;

Halleluiah, You are my Beloved,

    YOU ARE MY LOVE, YOU ARE MY ALL.

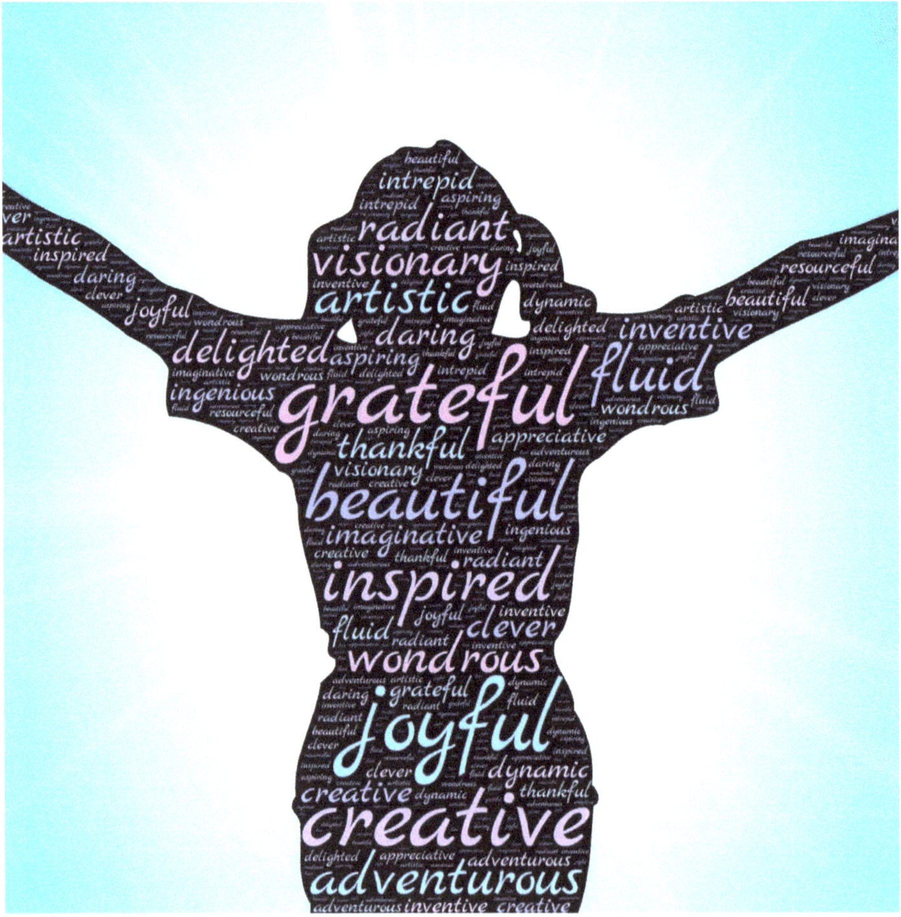
beautiful
intrepid
aspiring
intrepid
artistic
radiant
visionary
inspired
inspired
daring
clever
joyful
artistic
dynamic
daring
delighted
delighted
inventive
aspiring
wondrous
fluid
imaginative
ingenious
grateful
wondrous
resourceful
creative
thankful
appreciative
visionary
beautiful
imaginative
ingenious
creative
thankful
radiant
inspired
inventive
fluid
joyful
clever
radiant
wondrous
grateful
daring
joyful
clever
dynamic
creative
thankful
creative
delighted
appreciative
adventurous
adventurous
adventurous
inventive
creative
resourceful
beautiful

LET YOUR LIGHT SHINE
(Inspired by Matthew 5:13-16)

> "You are the salt of the earth...let your light shine before men; that they may see your good works, and glorify your Father who is in Heaven."
>
> —Matthew 5:13-16

*Lord, I am your servant and
I want to do Your will.
We are called to serve one another;
We are called to give love and
support, and
We are called to share our gifts of
talent and treasure.
We are called to love one another,
As God loves His church;
We are called to bring light and
peace to the world, not war.
We are called to be the salt of the
earth.*

"Love is the essence of life and without love, we are nothing. Without God, we are nothing."

Throughout history, man has constantly sinned and disobeyed God. Despite our sinfulness, God has shown His true mercy, compassion and power by bringing us out of the darkness and into the light. God continuously proves His love through the many blessings we receive each and every day. He also directs us, through the Holy Spirit that lives within us, to follow the path of righteousness and fulfill our life's purpose.

In order to fulfill one's purpose in life, however, it takes great courage and faith. As we all may have experienced in one time or another, life is not easy and we are faced with our share of contradictions and difficulties. We are faced with many challenges along the way and it is not easy to let go and surrender to God's will.

As we all know, life may also change unexpectedly, from one moment to the next. There are times we will experience difficult times and our faith will be challenged. In addition to these experiences or external sources, there are times that our own thoughts and fears can place limitations or hinder the blessings that God has in store for us.

I can certainly attest from my own personal experiences that with God, there are NO limits. Every person and living creature on this earth was created with a purpose and represents God. Every person on this earth represents God's love.

We must remember that God created us in His image and we are loved by our Creator. We must remember that life is special and it is a gift that we must treasure. *Love is the essence of life and without love, we are nothing. Without God, we are nothing.*

The world is a melting pot, filled with so much beauty and people of many languages, beliefs and cultures. Each person is unique and born with special inherent gifts that are to be cultivated and shared. We certainly do not have control over our families and the circumstances in which we are born. Perhaps our families did not have the means, knowledge or resources to cultivate, strengthen and encourage our gifts, but even with these limitations, God wants us to share our gifts of life, love, forgiveness and compassion with one another.

We are all called to love, serve and support one another. We are called to share our gifts of talent and treasure, no matter how great or small. Life is filled with many choices and possibilities. Although we are surrounded by negativity and there are evil forces that would like us to believe to the contrary, each person on this earth is loved by God and has free will.

One can choose to be the salt of the earth and bring flavor to a world that may be easily lost to the corruption of sin. We can also do our part in making this world a better place by choosing to become the best versions of ourselves, sharing the love and light that God has placed deep within our souls.

BE THE LIGHT.

ABOUT THE AUTHOR

Q. M. Herrera is a very spiritual person with a mature understanding of the core values of the Christian faith. Her passion for music and singing has been part of her spiritual journey since her childhood.

Q. M. Herrera discovered her love of writing during her collegiate studies at Kaplan University, where she attained her Master of Science in Legal Studies. She hopes to continue to bring love and inspiration to all through her music and inspirational writings.

www.ingramcontent.com/pod-product-compliance
Lightning Source LLC
Chambersburg PA
CBHW040328300426
44113CB00020B/2691